You Don't Have to Be DUMB to Be STUPID

You Don't Have to Be DUMB to Be STUPID

Bill Engvall
and David Brown

LONGSTREET PRESS
Atlanta, Georgia

Published by
LONGSTREET PRESS, INC.
A subsidiary of Cox Newspapers,
A subsidiary of Cox Enterprises, Inc.
2140 Newmarket Parkway
Suite 122
Marietta, GA 30067

Printed in the United States of America

3rd Printing, 1997

Library of Congress Card Catalog Number: 96-79799

ISBN: 1-56352-389-2

Electronic film prep by OGI, Forest Park, GA
Book design by Neil Hollingsworth
Jacket design by Audrey Graham
Cover photo by Dean Dixon

TO J.P. WILLIAMS FOR BREATHING
LIFE INTO MY CAREER AGAIN

TABLE OF CONTENTS

> # WARNING!
>
> **Use of this product may cause shortness of breath, or milk to spurt out your nose. In extreme cases, a busted gut may result. Discontinue use and consult your Mom immediately!**

I find it amazing that nearly every product we buy today is imprinted with those little "WARNING" labels. You know, "Discharging This Shotgun into Your Face Could Be Harmful or Fatal." It's obvious that most of us would know that. But for every silly product warning, you know that somewhere, some incredibly stupid person wrote the company a letter that began, "I pointed your shotgun at my face and . . ."

I prefer to think that truly stupid people are rare indeed. Most of us possess a reasonable amount of intelligence and common sense. And yet, even the most educated among us will occasionally do or say things that can only be described as *stupid*.

For example, a guy makes a left turn from the right lane, directly in front of you, causing you to slam on your brakes. Among the other, more colorful names you might call him would be "stupid."

"Did you see what that stupid guy did?" you would shout. Of course, the guy might be a rocket scientist with a Ph.D.

from Harvard. And yet, with one confused and irrational act, he's become nothing more than "a stupid guy" to anyone who happened to see the illegal turn.

You see, even a Harvard-grad can be stupid.

And that's really what this book is all about. Stupid things we all do every day — well, all right, maybe not *every* day — that defy all logic and intelligence. You know, the dumb thing you did that you prayed no one saw and you would never have to confess to.

The book's not meant to be demeaning or degrading to anyone, but if it comes across that way to you, perhaps you should check to see if your sign isn't just a little too tight.

THE SIGN

Stupid people are much more clever than most folks give them credit for. As masters of disguise, they blend naturally with almost any crowd. They can carry on intelligent conversations, drive flashy cars, wear expensive clothes. Heck, some even have college degrees and professional jobs. But don't be fooled; it's only a scam.

I'm convinced that stupid people spend most of their lives waiting for the opportunity to prey on unsuspecting normal people. It's like a contest. For example, if you get lost and accidentally ask a stupid person for directions, well, the stupid person figures that that makes you even stupider than he or she is. Score one for the stupid person!

So stupid people wait around, hiding, blending with their surroundings, hoping someone will mistake them for a normal person. Then, when a *real* normal person comes up and asks for help or directions, the stupid person pounces like a pig on a peanut, and say things like, "You can't get there from here," and "You know that road by the water tower? Don't take that one." Heaven help the poor sap!

To protect us ordinary, normal folks, stupid people ought to have to wear signs that say "I'm Stupid." That way they couldn't sneak up on you, and you'd never, ever have to depend on them for anything. If you inadvertently stopped a stupid person to ask directions, you'd quickly see their sign. Then, you could say, "Oh, wait a minute, I didn't see your sign. Never mind. I'll ask someone else."

As for all those goofy warning labels that are printed on every product we buy, well, they'd be history. You see, those labels aren't for folks like you and me; they're for stupid people. So if a clerk saw someone with a *Stupid sign*, he or she just wouldn't sell them the products.

For instance, did you know that on a tube of Preparation-H there is actually a warning that says "Do Not Take This Product Orally." Man, that's really sad! Can you imagine the letter that someone wrote the company?

> Dear Preparation-H:
>   I ate this whole tube of your product, and I still have those darned hemorrhoids.
>   And man, my mouth is so small, I can't even eat a jellybean. But, boy, I can whistle *real* good . . .

And you know it's true. Someone *really* wrote a letter like that. And bingo, a few days later, the warning label appeared on the product.

They should have just sent the poor idiot a sign!

Some of those labels just crack me up. I mean, did you know that on a blow dryer, there's a warning not to use the dryer while you are in the shower?

They're kidding, right? I mean, can you imagine standing in the shower, you've just finished shampooing your hair . . .

"Hey, Honey! Toss me that blow dryer, would you?"

Or another one on blow dryers that says, "Do Not Use This Product While Sleeping." Now hasn't *that* become a problem! I can't tell you how many times I've been sleeping away, and woke up to find myself doing my hair.

"Dang it! I was sleep-styling again!"

Somebody, somewhere is in serious need of a sign.

The next time you get your clothes back from the dry cleaner's, take a look at the bag. I swear, it says, "This Is Not a Toy."

Where the heck did that come from? Did they do a survey at the mall during Christmas? I mean, I can just see some youngster perched on Santa's lap: "No, Santa, I don't believe I want a bike or a train. . . . Heck, just a big old clear cleaning bag, that'd do for me."

Or how about the warning on shaving cream that says, "Avoid Spraying This Near an Open Flame."

Where the heck was *that* guy shaving? He must've been sitting around the campfire one night when he got to feeling a little bristly. "Hey, Bubba. Toss me that shaving cream. I believe I'm gonna freshen up before we turn in."

Did you know that on the back of a car fan-belt package, it actually says, "Stop Motor Before Applying This Product."

Wouldn't you have loved to have been there the first time *that* happened?

Some guy walks into the garage office, his hands are all cut-up and bloody. The boss says, "Hey, Walt, what happened, man?"

Walt looks up sheepishly as he applies a tourniquet to his arm and says, "Look here boys. Let me give y'all a little tip. If you're gonna put a fan belt on a car, you'd better shut the motor off first! You can't stop it with your hands, man. It's like a machine or something."

Speaking of cars, I had to see this one myself to believe it.

I was trying to sell my car a few months ago, and a guy came by to look at it. After he took it for a drive around the block, he stepped out of the car and reached down and *grabbed the exhaust pipe*!

"Darn, that's hot," he yelled, as he shook his hand wildly.

Now, if he had just been wearing a sign, I could have stopped him! I could have explained, "Now, I know you probably won't understand this, but don't grab the muffler, okay? It's gonna be really hot, and you don't want to touch it." Simple, right?

If you've ever bought a piece of electronic equipment, or even a pair of shoes, you've probably found a little packet of drying agent. And right there, for everyone to see, is a little warning label that says, "Do Not Eat This."

How many times have you ever bought a pair of shoes thinking that there just might be something to eat in there? But you just know that some lady, somewhere, opened up that shoebox and said, "Oh, looky! I got a pair of pumps *and* a pack of Chicklets!"

The evidence that stupid people are everywhere is overwhelming. While we feel their presence every day through ridiculous warning labels, they serve other more useful purposes. After all, if it weren't for stupid people, many of the scientific and technological breakthroughs that we enjoy today would still be ideas waiting to be tested. I'll give you a perfect example: shark-bite suits.

Just the other day, I was watching a program on one of the nature networks that was all about diving in the ocean. In one segment, the show explained how diving has become much less dangerous since the introduction of the shark-bite suit. This is a suit that is so tough that a shark cannot bite through it, and it will, therefore, prevent serious bodily injury to a diver in the event of an attack.

But you see, at some point, that was all just a theory. Then, one day, somewhere, some scientist had to actually *test* the suit, to see if the theory was fact. And that's where the stupid person came in to do us all a favor. I can just picture it: "Hey, Jimmy, c'mere," the scientist said. "Man, that shark suit looks real good on you. Now, here's what we're gonna do. We're gonna strap dead fish all over your body. Now, stay with me, Jimbo, stay with me. You just jump into this pool of sharks, and you tell us if it hurts when they bite you."

And you just know Jimbo would scratch his head and mumble, "Well, all right. But you'd better hold my sign. I don't want to lose it."

And so, today, divers everywhere can be thankful to Jimbo

for playing an important role in the development of a fine piece
of safety equipment.

The sad news is that the chances of encountering a stupid person in a critical situation are very high. My advice is to stay
calm and maintain a sense of superiority. One time last summer
when I was driving down the road I got a flat tire. Fortunately,
I was close to a gas station, so I just pulled the car into the lot
and stopped. An attendant walked out, looked at the tire, and
I swear, he said to me, "Tire go flat?"

I kept as straight a face as I could and replied, "No. Huh-uh.
I was just driving down the road, when all of the sudden, those
other three just swelled right up on me."

I figured that'd leave him stumped. But he never even batted
an eyelash. He just nodded his head and said, "Yep. The heat'll
do that."

What else could I say? I just reached into my briefcase and
handed him his very own sign. I figured it was the very least I
could do.

Then he looked at me suspiciously and asked, "Where's
yours?"

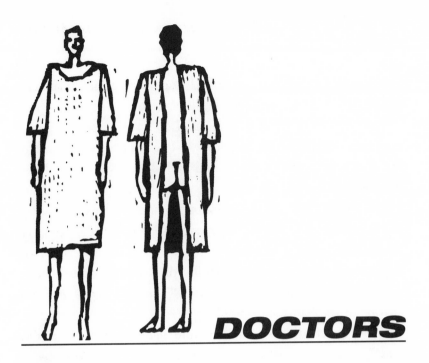

DOCTORS

I have always hated going to see the doctor, but that might sound really strange if you knew how many times a year I actually go there. You see, I am what they call "symptomatic," which means that if I hear symptoms, I'll make myself *believe* I have the disease.

Once at a party, a friend of mine who also is a comedian slipped up to me real casually, looked around to make certain no one could overhear him, and asked, "Hey, Bill, what are the symptoms of herpes?"

I just shuddered. "I don't know. Now shut up."

I tried valiantly to close him out, not to hear another word, but he persisted.

"You itch, don't you?" he asked innocently enough. "*Down there.*"

I just threw my head back in anguish, groaning, and walked away. Sure enough, not five minutes later I started to itch. *Down there.*

"Great!" I thought to myself. "I've got herpes, all right. I'm itching. *Now* what the heck am I gonna do?"

So I went to the doctor. And yes, I *do* have a reserved parking place there now. Heaven knows, I've *paid* for it. He asked me what was wrong this time, and I told him. "Well, Doc. I got the big 'H.'"

"Hemorrhoids?" he said, looking genuinely concerned.

"No, I ate that tube of Preparation-H. I've got herpes," I whispered.

He stroked his chin thoughtfully for a minute, and then he looked right into my eyes and asked, "Bill, have you slept with anyone other than your wife?"

I was shocked! "No, sir. I would *never* do anything like that!"

He smiled. "Well, Bill, there's no way you've got herpes, then."

I was not so easily convinced.

"Hey, Doc," I said looking around carefully. "I'm itching. You know, *down there.*"

After a quick examination — although I must say when one man is examining another man's private parts, there is no such thing as a *quick* examination — he made his diagnosis.

"You've got a simple heat rash," he said. And then, he asked me, "Bill, do you dust your balls?"

At first I was just stunned. I was certain I must have heard him wrong. I said, "I'm sorry, Doc," as I choked back the laughter. "I could've sworn you just asked me if I dusted my balls. What would I be checking for? Fingerprints?"

He never said a word. Just stared at me with that look that says, "I'm a doctor. I never kid around, so cut it out."

But I couldn't resist. "Yeah, I tried Pledge but it left a waxy build-up."

Without so much as a smile, he tore off my prescription and handed it to me. I was about to find out what a good ball-dusting was all about.

As embarrassing as *that* trip to the doctor's office was, even worse was when the family was vacationing and I had to visit a strange doctor. Not strange in the weird sense, just strange in that I'd never *been* to this particular doctor before.

My family had been spending a lot of time in the swimming pool, and apparently my skin reacted to the chlorine in the water. There was some flaking going on where there just shouldn't have been. I know. I looked it up in my handy family medical encyclopedia. By the way, you should never travel without one. Anyhow, I looked it up, and it just said, "No. Go see a doctor, *now*, Bill."

Always an adventurous spirit, I grabbed the phone book and pulled a name out of the hat, so to speak. I figured one doctor was as good as the next, so what the heck was the difference? When I first got there, I had to spend twenty minutes filling out routine paperwork, insurance stuff and the like. But when I got to the part which asked, "Why are you here?" I got a little nervous. I mean, I didn't want to *write it down*, for heaven's sake. It's one thing to tell a doctor in the privacy of an examining room, but that *paperwork* floats all over the office.

I could just picture the nurses shuffling it back and forth, arguing with one another.

"I'm not going to touch him. You take him in there."

"Not me. It's your turn. Shhhhhhh! Here he comes . . ."

Heck, even the secretaries and bookkeepers probably read

the interesting ones. So I decided to try and put down what I thought was the medical terminology for my problem. Let me give you a tip, folks. Don't ever do this. Because then, they know you're an idiot, right off the bat.

So, after thinking about my problem for a few minutes, I finally hit on what I felt was the correct medical term. I wrote, "Eczema of the cucumbus-majoris."

I then quickly shuffled the paper to the bottom of the stack, and handed it back to the nurse. Before I could even turn to walk away, she had found the paper and looked at what I wrote.

"What the heck is that?" she asked without introduction.

"Well, the *doctor* will know," I said haughtily. "Maybe you missed that day in school." Then I strode back to my seat without another word.

A few minutes later I was escorted into the examining room, and sat down to wait for the doctor. Now, remember, I had just picked a name out of the phone book, so I was just expecting some old geezer to show up.

So who walks through the door? A knock-out, 38-year-old brunette lady-doctor. I thought, "Aw, man! Not *this* time!!"

Face it, I had dreamed of that situation all my life. You know, where I'd be sick, but not *too* sick. And me and the lady-doctor would talk, have some wine, hold hands . . .

Anyway, this gorgeous lady-doctor looked over my paperwork, and the warm smile slowly faded from her face. Finally, she looked up at me and asked, "Mr. Engvall?"

I felt like a kid in school caught throwing spitballs. I meekly raised my hand and said, "Here."

"I give up," she said, shrugging her shoulders. "Just what, exactly, is a 'cucumbus-majoris'?"

The little kid in me just wouldn't go away. I shuffled my feet and stared at the ceiling.

"You know," I squeaked.

From the confused look on her face, I could see that she *didn't* know. So I helped her out by pointing quickly to my crotch, then looking away again. That time, the light came on in the doctor's library.

"Oh, for goodness sake, Mr. Engvall. Why don't you just call it by its name?"

I gave her that you've-got-to-be-kidding look, and said, "Like you would have understood 'Big Wally'?"

Eventually, I cured the problem. But the doctor wanted to know if she could surgically attach my sign so that it would *never* fall off again.

Medical emergencies happen. Sometimes you just get sick, and you soon realize that no amount of chicken soup and aspirin is going to make you better. So, you go to the doctor. But at least once a year, you know well in advance that you're going. And usually, you aren't even sick.

You know what I'm talking about — your annual physical.

Now, most of the stuff you go through is pretty routine. Filling out questionnaires, blood pressure checks, pulse rate and stuff. It's when they get to the urine sample that things start to go downhill. Actually, it wouldn't be quite so bad if the bathroom wasn't always on one side of the waiting room and the lab on the other. They make you carry that tiny clear cup all the way across the room. And you're just praying that you don't spill it, or run into someone you know who might want to stop you to chat or gossip.

As much as I hate needles, I believe I'd rather have blood taken from my arm than suffer through a prostate exam. Interestingly enough, however, they usually manage to do *both* during the course of my physical.

Fellas, you know what I'm talking about, don't you? Just when you think he's about done, and you're hoping that maybe this year he forgot — he pulls out his little *rubber glove*. You sit on the table and smile, pretending that you don't know what's about to happen. While the doctor *studies* his little glove, wriggling his fingers all around to make sure it works right, I guess.

Ladies, I don't even want to guess what it's like for y'all. But most men would rather charge an enemy machine-gun nest armed with a squirt-gun than bend over for a doctor wearing a rubber glove.

The last time I had one of these things, I don't know what this fellow was looking for, but after a while I said, "Hey, Doc. Why don't you tell me what I'm *thinking*?"

He paused, leaned over so he could see the side of my face, which I thought was polite, and asked, "Why?"

"'Cause you're touching my brain, man!" I whimpered. "That's my cerebrum there, E.T., and if you're checking for cavities, heck, I've got a dentist, thanks."

And, to add insult to injury, as it were, they always use that . . . *stuff*. You know, it's like axle grease in a tube. You can't wash that stuff off with Lava soap and an S.O.S. pad. For the rest of the day, you're walking around with that *gushy* feeling in your shorts, and no matter how hard you try, you can't help but walk funny. Other guys look at you and say, "Got the finger, huh?"

The worst part of it was that after he had finished his exam, the doctor asked, "Is there anything else I need to know?"

I looked at him with a tear in my eye and that just-lost-my-virginity look and uttered the only words that came to mind: "Call me."

IN-VITRO FERTILIZATION

People are always reminiscing on "the good ol' days," and how wonderful things used to be when life was a lot simpler. But I, for one, am thankful for a lot of things modern technology has brought about.

Can you imagine life today without the convenience of a microwave oven, or for many of us, the computer? But I am especially grateful for the advances in medicine.

I have two children, a girl and a boy. The girl is the oldest, and she came to us quite naturally. But to have the boy, we had to use what can only be described as a miracle of modern medicine — in-vitro fertilization.

While I am amazed that this procedure is even possible, and very grateful for the wonderful son it produced for us, I have to admit that it was the most humiliating procedure I have ever participated in.

Before we could even begin, I had to go in for a little test. You know, to make sure I was *packing a loaded gun.*

Basically, I had to go to the clinic at seven in the morning and . . . *butter the corn.* And as embarrassing as that was, when I got there I had to wait in line! There were like eight guys ahead of me.

Talk about uncomfortable. I mean, everybody knows why the other fellow is there, so there's absolutely *nothing* to talk about.

"What are you doing here?"

"Aw, I just came by to look at the magazines." Yeah, right.

When it was finally my turn, the nurse called my name and handed me a jar about the size of a jumbo mayonnaise container. All I could do was laugh.

"Well, I guess you've heard the rumor, huh?" I said, trying to inject some humor into the situation. "Step back, fellas. I don't want anybody gettin' hurt."

Of course the nurse had *no* sense of humor. "Give us what you can," she growled.

She led me to an office and explained that in the bathroom I would find a television, a VCR, and a porno movie.

I said, "Gee, I hope it isn't one I've already seen!" More unappreciated humor.

Nurse Ratchet just shook her head and replied, "Shut up."

Then, she locked me in the bathroom and left. It was then that I really started having mixed feelings about the whole thing.

Picture this . . . well, maybe you *shouldn't.* Anyway, I'm standing there with my pants down around my ankles, holding this jar and watching a porno movie. And all I could think of right then was, if somebody were to open the door, I'd be going to jail.

The whole time I was in there, I had two thoughts racing

through my mind: (1) "I just want to get this over with," and (2) "I don't want to come out of here *too* quick." After all, I have my pride! You sure as heck don't want to open that door and hear, "Whewee! There's a record!" You might see a lighted scoreboard in the lobby where they are flashing your time. And some guy is saying, "I'll never beat that! That guy's a professional!"

Anyway, after what I felt to be an appropriate amount of time, I emerged with my sample. Now, I'm not sure how they grade it, maybe on some kind of a curve or something. But I passed. So we got to move on to the next phase.

A week later they called me and told me I had to come back in to fertilize the eggs.

So I got to the clinic at seven in the morning again. The same guys as before were waiting in the lobby — we've formed a bowling league now. We call it "Buttered Veggies." Anyway, the nurse finally called my name and gave me my jar. I headed right for the bathroom, popped the movie in and fast-forwarded to where I left off. (Hey, you miss a second of those movies, and you're lost in the plot forever!)

When I finished, I gave my specimen to the nurse, and went to sit in the lobby to wait for the results. Not ten minutes later, she came out holding another jar.

"Mr. Engvall," she said, "We're going to need *some more*."

"*Now* there's pressure!"

So I went back into the bathroom, and somehow managed to do it *twice* in ten minutes. I was *very* proud of myself. Of course, my wife was not too pleased.

"At home, you're One-Shot Johnnie," she whined. "But put you in a Texaco bathroom and 'Mr. Stud' appears."

I went back out to the waiting area. There was this one poor guy who just couldn't do it. The guy was in the bathroom for something like forty minutes. Now, at that point, all us regulars were pretty impressed. Either this guy was some kind of a stud, or there was a *really* good movie that week. We weren't sure.

It turned out to be neither. He came out with a whipped-dog look on his face and said, "I couldn't do it." We showed what we felt was the proper degree of sympathy — we all laughed!

"Step aside, Rookie," one of the regulars said as he pushed out his chest and headed into the bathroom.

I was thinking, "Take a seat on the bench, kid. Let me show you how a professional does it."

Thankfully, all the humiliation was well worth the effort. We were soon blessed with a fine, healthy son. And now, I've got a great family — a lovely wife and two wonderful children. But I sure wore out my sign at that doctor's office.

KIDS

The only thing that has given me a bigger thrill than buying my first truck was becoming a father. Having children truly makes the meaning of life a simple question to answer. Children are the joy and light of the world.

One of the great things about children is their chameleon-like mood-swings. Just when they have pushed you to the edge of the envelope, they can bring you back in a second with a simple smile or a laugh. But for all the wonder that children bring into our lives, they can also cause us the most frustration and anguish, at times, too.

I've found one of the most annoying habits kids have is, they never forget a promise. They catch you late at night, tired from a long day of fighting with the boss, and all you want to do is to collapse on the sofa and watch "Rifleman" reruns with a cold beer.

"Daddy, Daddy," they yell exuberantly as they sail across the room and land in your lap. "Take me to the park."

And as much as part of you might want to do that, a bigger part of you is *not* getting off that sofa. (After all, this is the episode where Lucas is temporarily blinded by a bullet and must learn to shoot relying only on his sense of hearing.) So, you explain that you're really tired and, "We'll do it *tomorrow*, Honey." And what you're really hoping is that, by tomorrow, they'll have forgotten all about it.

But they never do, do they? Nope. And you want to know why? It's because they are like little court reporters taking down every single word. Oh, you may not see the machine, but it's there somewhere. That's the only way I can figure that they can remember *every* word you say, from cuss words to promises!

I learned this lesson the hard way. One morning my daughter came in and asked when we were leaving for Disneyland.

"Huh?" I stammered.

"You said you'd take us to Disneyland today," she continued, undaunted.

"No, I didn't," I said, hoping that I hadn't, while knowing that I probably had but hoping I could talk her out of it.

"Yes, you did. Three weeks ago at the dinner table you said you'd take us to Disneyland *today*." And despite the puzzled look on my face she continued, "Maybe if you'd *review the transcripts* it would refresh your memory!"

We had a ball at Disneyland that day....

But my daughter, who is now nine years old is just getting to that age where she is starting to adopt grown-up mannerisms. But she's still not sure how they all work. And she has begun using certain little behaviors which can be either really cute, or just plain annoying as heck.

One of her more annoying tricks is when you say something to her that she thinks is beneath her, she crosses her arms and sucks her teeth, making a sound like a pacifier being yanked from a baby's mouth. When this happens, I think, "Boy, I sure hope you're sucking stuff out of your teeth...."

Another one happened just the other night. I told her that before she could watch any more television, she had to finish her homework. She dropped her hands to her sides, screwed her face into a retarded expression, and said, "Well, *duhh*."

Oh, yeah! That really *lit* me up!!

They should just take that duhh-word right out of the English language, because some kid is going to get hurt *really* bad.

Somewhere, sometime, a parent is going to come home, tired and annoyed from a pain-in-the-butt boss that's been riding him all day. The kid is going to say, "Well, duhh," and the next sound the neighbors hear will be a kid crashing through a wall.

"Well, I'm sorry, Your Honor," the parent would explain the next day in court. "But he said the D-word...."

If the judge is a *parent*, it might just be grounds for a dismissal.

Truth is, I just don't know where our age group went wrong as parents, but we're raising a whole generation of jackasses, you know. Kids today have no respect for anything, do they?

I think the problem is, parents today don't discipline their kids any more. And I can almost understand that, since they figure if they spank their kids, they, the parents, will go to jail. And as sad as that is, it's the truth.

Well, I'm sorry, but all the high-tech, sophisticated, psychological child-rearing techniques that have been formulated over the past twenty years are no substitute for a good old-fashioned ass-whipping.

Here's an example of what I mean. My wife and I went out to dinner recently with some friends of ours who use what they call "enlightened child-discipline techniques." I've figured out what that means is — never lay a hand on their children.

While we were eating dinner, their little boy went bananas! I understand about boys, because I've got one myself, but this kid was just plain being a turd! At first, his mother simply tried to explain it away by saying, "Oh, he's just *expressing* himself."

Of course, I was thinking that it was going to be one *very* long dinner. See, I was raised a little differently. When *we* went out to dinner with our folks, we could talk, amuse ourselves quietly in our seats and such. But we never, ever acted up, because we sure didn't want to hear Dad say, "You want me to take you outside?"

"No, sir!" we'd respond. Because we knew that *outside* there were *no witnesses*!

One time of being dragged out by an earlobe, past a grinning maitre'd, to the parking lot, was all it took to make me realize that I *never* wanted to go through *that* again.

But when my wife and our friends were sitting in that restaurant, this little boy stood up in his chair and just started *screaming* at the top of his lungs. Man, I started going through D.T.'s. My whole body was shaking like a junky needing a fix. I was thinking, "Hey, if you're not feeling up to it, *I'll* kill him for you."

His mother, however, handled it like this. She pointed at him and said, "Billy, if you don't use your *indoor* voice, you're going to get a *time-out*."

Time-out? Shoot, I was thinking what that boy needed was a *knock*-out.

Do you know what a time-out is? That's when a kid who's done something wrong is placed in a chair. Then, he has to sit there and *think* about what he's done.

Now where was *that* when we were kids?

"Oh, yeah, Dad. I'm thinking about it," we'd have chuckled. "I'll never do *that* again, I promise. Heh, heh, heh."

After the dinner episode, I found myself frequently having arguments with my friend's wife. She thinks that spanking is cruel and unusual punishment and I don't think it is. And no matter how much we debate the issue, neither of us will budge on our opinions.

Now, to my way of thinking, cruel and unusual punishment was when my Dad used to make us go outside and cut our own switch. You know, a thin little twig used to get a message across.

Now *that* is cruel and unusual punishment!

The whole time you were out there staring at that tree, you'd be thinking, "Oh, man. If I pick that little one, he's just going to send me right back out here. And that one there is going to break my spine. And that one ..."

And while you were out there anguishing over which twig to pick, you knew your parents were inside watching you and just laughing their butts off!

I got sent out to that tree so often as a boy that pretty soon it was nothing more than a barren stump. The neighbors thought there was some kind of tree disease going around.

Another form of cruel and unusual punishment is the simple sound of a belt clearing belt-loops. Anyone over thirty will remember that sound well.

The only sound worse than a belt coming out was the sound Dad made if the belt got snagged and didn't come all the way out on the first tug. When he made that little *grunting* sound, I knew I wouldn't be sitting down for a week!

I make no apologies. I think spanking is a necessary tool of parenting, provided it is used sparingly and with a clear head. After all these years, I finally figured out why Dad made us go cut switches; it was so he would have time to cool off before administering our whippings. And the Good Lord knows, I'm grateful for that.

Many of our problems with young people might be avoided if more parents would simply employ the time-proven method of spanking. I'll tell you how effective it can be:

Remember that young man who was *caned* over in Singapore for spray-painting cars? (I was singing the Singapore National Anthem, that day!) I guarantee you, he won't be spray-painting any more cars!! Heck, I'll bet he doesn't even take an *art class* at school.

Now, if I were his father, I'd have gone over there to Singapore and bought that bamboo stick they used in his punishment. I'd have brought it home and hung it up over the door in the boy's bedroom.

Then, every time the kid started screwing around, I could just point to it and say, "Watch it, boy. Don't *make* me call Mr. Fuji! You know I will *gladly* pay his airfare...."

Kids today just don't get enough ass-whippings. Of course, if *society* was the same back when we were kids as it is today, all our parents would have gone to jail for life. I don't know about you, but I *got* some ass-whippings when I was growing up. But I have to admit, they were not undeserved — it was ass-whipping material!

I remember when they first introduced "unbreakable" bottles. My mother brought home a big bottle of Scope mouthwash in a plastic bottle that said "Unbreakable!" right across the front.

I just figured it was a *dare*. It was time for the "home-test." My sister and I took that bottle into the bathroom and started *flinging* it against the bathroom wall, hitting it on the bathtub and stuff. And it was tough, I'll admit. It wouldn't break ... until I flung it at the doorknob.

Boy, that was an ass-whipping I'll never forget.

And then there was the time I got the "Hall of Fame" ass-whipping. What happened was, my mom and dad were doing the dishes after dinner one night. They got into a little water fight, flicking dishwater on each other. I realize *now* it was just *foreplay*, but at the time I didn't have a clue.

Anyway, being young and dumb, I figured I should be right in the middle of that water fight. So I flicked some water on my mother. But this woman *knew* how to water-fight. She scooped a big iced-tea glass full of water and just doused me with it. I was so startled, I just stepped back and glared at her. But what got me into trouble was when I muttered, "I'm gonna *kill* you."

Fortunately, that's about all I remember. I never even saw my Dad's hand coming. I *do* remember thinking that I was going to mess my pants, though. As hard as he was whipping me, I figured just the suction from his hand being drawn back would pull the crap right out of my butt! But I also knew that if I crapped in my pants, it would just make him even madder than he was.

Another thing kids learn early about ass-whippings is never to put their hands behind their bottoms. Around my house, if one of us put his hands behind himself, he just bought an extra 30 minutes of ass-whipping. Dad hated it, because it really threw off his timing.

Remembering the way things were back then, I often wish I could have been a parent 20 years ago instead of today. Parents back then didn't have any of the crap to worry about that parents do today. Take, for example, Halloween.

When I was a kid, Halloween was the best night of the year, except maybe for Christmas. Me and some of my buddies used to go out, all by ourselves, for five or six hours. Oh, sure, we might have gotten into a little mischief, but we never did anything that couldn't be washed off the next morning.

And we'd collect a whole pillowcase full of candy that didn't even have to be X-rayed before we ate it. In fact, most of it never even made it back to the house. We'd run around the neighborhood with our mouths stuffed so full of candy we looked like a bunch of chipmunks gathering nuts.

Here's another thing I recall from back then. No one had ever heard of a child's car seat. I remember playing a game, when the car was going 70 miles per hour, we'd jump up and down on the front seat. And we had *metal dashboards* back then!

Kids in our day just learned how to take a fall, for crying out loud. And capped teeth were much more popular back then than they are today. It was sort of like a status symbol to have your front teeth capped when I was a kid.

And the closest thing to air bags we had was Dad's arm! He'd slam on the brakes, we'd go flying ... but we almost never hit anything, except Dad's arm! Of course, I can't tell you how many split lips and bloody noses that arm caused, but it was all great fun!

"Aw, heck, you're not gonna die. Just tip your head back and sit down," he'd say as he spun gravel getting back out on the road again.

I remember another car game we used to play when I was a kid. We'd take turns lying up in the back, scrunched up against the window. It was so cool! You could pick your nose as a cop drove past. Or yank your arm up and down as a semi-truck pulled up behind you so he would blow his air horn. And when he did, Dad would flip him off! Then, the truck would dog you for a few miles trying to run you off the road.

It was great fun!

I'll always treasure the memory of Dad slamming on the brakes when I was lying in that backseat window. I'd go flying through the air, hit the front seat and crumple to the floor-board. When I got my breath back, I always climbed back up there and begged him to do it again.

I never once remember fastening a seat belt as a kid. In fact, I don't even remember *seeing* one. My dad used to cut them out of the car as soon as we'd get it home from the car lot.

Of course, the way the laws are today, you'd have to be wearing a *Stupid* sign *not* to wear a seat belt. Can you say "$75 ticket"?!

PARENTING

It would have been a whole lot easier being a parent back when we were kids, but I guess the changing times are something we simply have to accept. Things today are what they are. But I wish somebody would have told me at least a *few* things about being a parent.

For instance, no one ever told me that you can't pass gas around a kid. I had to find that out on my own. You see, a kid just can't keep a secret.

"I smell poo-poo, Daddy," they wail in a siren-like voice — in the grocery store.

Also there is no way to be a parent and keep even a shred of personal dignity. And here's the proof of that. A few years ago, we had to potty-train my son. We got him to that point where he would go on his own, but he just couldn't finish the paper-work. Whenever he had concluded his business, he'd climb off the toilet and yell, "Dad! I'm done!" That translates to, "Wipe my butt!" When you walk into that bathroom and he's "assumed the position," any dignity you might have had is gone forever.

Another thing I wish I had known about before becoming a parent is that you must handle like an expert situations you could never plan for. For example, one night, my two kids were taking a bath when I heard this blood-curdling scream. I glanced up from my *Modern Parent* magazine (okay, I made up that part), and it looked like someone had *shot* my daughter out of the tub from a cannon. Before I could even ask her what the problem was, I saw the *turd* floating in the bathwater. And while my daughter was screaming and running around like someone had just thrown nuclear acid on her, my son, proud of his accomplishment, wanted to stay in the tub and play with his turd.

"Look, Daddy! Big boat!" he giggled as it floated around.

When I tried to get him out of the tub, he got all upset because he didn't understand why he couldn't stay in there and play with the boat. Finally, after much calm and rational discussion, I got both kids out of the tub. It was then I faced one of those interesting parent-dilemmas that no one ever tells you about. I had to figure out whether to drain the tub first or capture it as it floated around in the bathwater.

I always thought that there should be a parenting book that covered stuff like this. Then I could have just hollered at my wife, "Honey, look up 'Poop in the Bathtub' and tell me what it says, all right?" (By the way, if this ever happens to you, the answer is you drain the tub first. I know. I tried it both ways.)

Another thing I've noticed about being a parent is that you can kiss your privacy good-bye. I fully understand now why my father used to lock the bathroom door. He wasn't embarrassed about anything; it was the only time he ever got to be alone.

Even with the door locked, however, you still can't get away from those little hands that somehow manage to slip *under* the bathroom door to wave at you. And not far away is a little eyeball peering at your feet.

"Whatcha doin', Dad?"

"I'm building a rocket," you answer. "Now get the heck out of here!"

"Well, I wanna see the rocket ..."

I remember one morning, I was taking a shower. I had the bathroom door shut, but somehow I had forgotten to lock it. All of the sudden, the shower curtain was ripped back, and there stood my daughter with her friend!

Next thing I knew, the girls were marching back out the door, and my daughter huffed, "See? I told you."

I never found out what that was all about, but I'll tell you something I did learn that day: There is absolutely no way for a wet, naked man to climb a tile wall. It just can't be done.

My daughter is at that age where she is just starting to figure stuff out. Usually, she is polite enough to leave us out of her wonderings, but occasionally, she'll come and ask a question.

The other day, just after breakfast, she came into the kitchen and asked, "Dad, what is sex?"

After I spit coffee all over the counter, I had to peel my wife off the ceiling! She kept saying, "I told you she saw us! I told you so!"

My wife freaked out so bad I thought I was going to have to slap her face just to get her to control herself! Funny how that always works in the movies, but in real life it just gets you a couple of days in jail.

Anyway, so my little girl was looking at her mother trying to figure out why she was so upset. I lovingly put my hand on her head and asked her, "Where did you hear about this?"

She said, "Daddy, my friend at school said that sex is when a man and woman kiss, and then wrestle around."

I figure it all depends on how well you wrestle, but that definition was as good as any I'd heard from a nine year-old, and I told her so.

The one thing I've found to be even worse than having your kids ask questions about sex is if they actually catch you in the act. Not that this happens very often. But even *one time* can lead to emotional distress that can last a lifetime. The kids handle it fine, but the *parents* are toast.

The one thing I can gratefully say about the one time we got caught is that, fortunately, we were under the covers. I mean, if the kid had been five minutes earlier, I might have still been swinging from the chandelier or something. Thank God for small favors!

I could picture that. Just as I swing naked across the room on the light fixture, my kid walks in and freezes in the doorway.

"Whatcha doin', Dad?"

"Changing a light bulb?" I might venture.

"Naked?" she'd respond.

"I didn't want my clothes to catch on fire," I'd cover, and hope she bought it. "If a light bulb blows up, my clothes would catch on fire just like a match! Poof! You change a light bulb, you've always got to be thinking about safety."

Anyway, back to the fateful day we got caught. It was one of those rare weekend mornings when we both woke up feeling just a little bit amorous. I tip-toed out to check on the kids, and they were watching cartoons, oblivious to the world. So I sneaked back into the bedroom and crawled up under the cov-ers for a lightning round in the wrestling ring.

My wife and I were completely engrossed in what we were doing, when I suddenly felt this little tapping on the back of my head.

My first thought was, "I know my wife is not *that* limber." And then, the lights came on in my brain, and panic set in. I jerked my head around and my worst nightmare came to life — there stood my kid.

After a few minutes of awkward explanations as to why we couldn't get out of bed at that *exact* moment, we finally con-vinced her to go have a seat at the table and that one of us would be along directly to fix breakfast.

Needless to say, that was the *last time* we ever attempted love-making while the sun was up.

But my daughter never suspected a thing. Or at least we don't think she did. Of course, she's only nine, so the subject may come up again in another ten or fifteen years. But at least we have that long to *think* we pulled one over on her.

As I said, my daughter is full of questions. And that is a good thing, I figure, because I was always taught that a curious mind is an intelligent mind.

But what scares me is that now my daughter can *read*. So she doesn't need to ask us everything, she can just find it out on her

own. In some cases, that's great. But there are other times, we
wonder just *where* she learned certain things.

"I read it," she'd say smugly.

And while my daughter constantly amazes us with her intel-
lectual aptitude and educational prowess, my son is just *learning* to read. And he's really testing parental patience to the
limit.

I never thought I would ever cuss Dr. Seuss, but after you've
read *The Cat in the Hat*, say, forty times, it's inevitable. When
you see your kid race into the room with that book under his
arm, you think up some brand-new expletives to describe Dr.
Suess's ancestors. Anymore, I see a kid's book and fifteen minutes later I've got a beer in one hand and a cigarette in the
other.

And the trick is, you can't just read the book *to* your child,
you have to let *them* read it. Pretty soon, I'm like a Dallas
Cowboys cheerleader. And it's not just because I like to wear
white boots and short-shorts. I start coaxing him along, hoping
he'll make that long-yardage play where he accidentally skips a
few pages.

"You can do it!" I cheer as he struggles with a word or
phrase.

But as the hours *drag* along it turns into, "No, it's 'Go, dog,
go! Go, dog, go!' for crying out loud. You just said it two pages
ago! Memory, son, memory!"

And just about that time is when my wife walks through the
door.

"What's going on in here?" she demands.

Then *I* become the four year-old. "Nothin'. We're just
readin'. Duhh."

I can't wait until he starts school, so I can let his teachers take over where I left off. Hopefully they can undo the damage I've done before it becomes a permanent learning disability. I am very grateful to teachers for the enormity of the tasks they face each day, and the good job they routinely do of educating our youngsters.

But the one thing I hate about school is the fact that every other day, it seems, my daughter is bringing home some new little gizmo or gadget to sell to raise money for this or that at school. They are turning our kids into little Amway people, man!

In the few years my daughter has been in school, we've sold more stuff than a Wal-Mart store. We've handled candy bars, wrapping paper, wall paper, you name it. Right now, we've got a whole case of light bulbs in the closet. And the thing about these light bulbs is, they're made by *blind* people.

I'm sorry, but that's just cruel. I mean, how do the blind people know if they work or not? Think about it. They've got to grab onto them and see if they're hot!

"Yee-ouch! This 'un works. Box it up, ship it...."

And when the kids sell these light bulbs, the money goes back to the blind people. Now that's a great cause, and I support the concept fully — except when I'm out there going door-to-door with my daughter. Then, I *hate* it.

The only good thing is, I've gotten to know all my neighbors now. Of course, most of them don't like me, and many actually hide when I knock on their doors. But when they *do* answer, I'm forced to recite the sales speech:

"Hi, I'm Bill. This is my daughter. We're selling light bulbs to help the blind people...."

And then my daughter throws in *her* little bit:

"But be sure to take off your clothes before you screw them in! Always think safety around light bulbs!"

Kids are great, aren't they?

And there's a big difference between raising girls and boys. I'm convinced that my little boy is going to make me pay for every rotten thing I ever did to my parents when I was growing up. Because now he's doing them to me!

Another thing about boys, I swear, I never thought I'd ever say these words, "Son, please don't bite the dog." But I say them all the time!

Our dog is so neurotic he won't even come out from under the couch unless my son is in bed.

"No, Bill, not as long as that little monster is still up," the dog says. "I'm staying right under this couch! I mean, just look at me! I look like I've got mange, for Pete's sake."

So when he can't drag the dog out from under the sofa, my son likes to play with his little plastic army-men. They came in a bucket, 250 little soldiers, in various poses, all ready to kill or maim the enemy.

The manufacturer claims that they are harmless toys. Obviously he never got up in the middle of the night to go to the bathroom, and stepped on one of those "harmless" soldiers!

That happened to me recently. And when I flipped on the light, I found that my son had placed his "I.G. Joes," as he calls them, in strategic locations all around my bedroom floor. With the light off, it would have been like trying to walk through a mine field.

There was even one positioned by the bathroom door, holding his little gun up menacingly, like he was guarding it.

"You here to wipe the general's butt?" he said. "All right. You can pass."

Inevitably, every couple of days or so, my son comes to me and asks me where all of his "I.G. Joes" are.

"Son, they're *everywhere*," I say in exasperation. "This house looks like the beaches of Normandy on D-Day."

So, every now and again, we get the bucket and go looking for all the men. Used to, no matter how many we found, they never seemed to fill the bucket back up. And we couldn't come up with any explanation for the missing-in-action ... until the day my wife decided to strip the wax off the kitchen floor.

When I moved the stove out from the wall, we found around fifty soldiers hiding under there. It was like we'd liberated the I.G. Joe Prison Camp.

Turns out, the cat didn't like stepping on the I.G. Joes, either. So anytime one would recon the kitchen floor, the cat would bat it around until it wound up under the stove.

Me and Kitty have gotten a lot closer since that day....

Little Boys and Barbie Dolls

'm convinced that my son figures his job in life is simply to destroy his sister's stuff. That's the job he applied for. He does stuff to a Barbie Doll that, well, you can't even laugh at.

We had a big blowout recently when he got into her room and tore up one of her Fashion Barbies. My daughter was madder than heck. I was too, since it's a $35 doll.

I've never understood why he doesn't tear up his own stuff. Heck, I'd *pay* him to tear up the Barney doll. I've watched enough Barney tapes that just seeing that stuffed doll makes me want to put a gun barrel in my mouth.

I'm convinced that Barney is the reason all the other dinosaurs are extinct. They saw him and said, "Man, we'd rather be dead than hang out with you."

Anyway, I know why *I* was mad; I'm the one who paid for the Fashion Barbie in the first place. But I don't understand why *my daughter* was mad. After all, it's not like it was her only Barbie Doll. Man, she's got every Barbie known to mankind. She's got Malibu Barbie, Surfing Barbie, Thanksgiving Barbie. She's even got Barbie on roller-blades.

To tell you the truth, I really hate Barbie Dolls. They're just too fluffy and frilly for my taste. I think they ought to come out with a more realistic Barbie Doll. Why isn't there a "White-Trash Barbie"?

This is Barbie in her later years. The modeling career is over, and Barbie and Ken live in a Barbie trailer-house. They could call it the "Dream Trailer." That Corvette would be on blocks in the front yard, with the fenders mashed in and the back window shot out.

Of course, Ken would have a big old beer belly, wear dirty white tee-shirts and spend a lot of his time scratching himself and belching.

"What's for supper tonight, Barbie?"

Barbie'd stick her head out the screen door, hair in curlers, and say, "Fish sticks."

Ken would probably grin and say, "Fish sticks? What? Is it our anniversary again?"

And imagine all the accessories you'd have to go along with White Trash Barbie. You could have a little police car that would pull up in front of the mobile home from time to time, because Ken got drunk and started yelling at Barbie.

Then, the cops could lead Ken off in some little Ken-Cuffs. Meanwhile, Ken would still be yelling at Barbie, "I know you slept with G.I. Joe! I know you did!"

And Barbie would be crying, sitting on the wooden steps, "Oh, don't take him away. I love him. He didn't mean it, I know he didn't."

My son is at that age where he often wakes up in the middle of the night and sneaks into our room. Truthfully, I don't mind most of the time. Heck, it usually doesn't even wake me up when he slips in between my wife and me and goes back to sleep. I know it's one of those precious things that we'll look back on in later years and remember fondly.

But the other night was that rare time when I objected in the strongest terms to having him in bed with us. At about 4:00 a.m., he got sick and barfed all over the bed.

It was at that exact moment I realized that they should make an alarm clock that sounds like a baby barfing. Because I guarantee, there'd be no 'snoozing.' You could be in the deepest R.E.M. sleep, drooling on yourself, but when that baby barfs, you would be off the bed in a heartbeat!

"Get up, get up, GET UP!" you'd scream in a panic. "Is it on me? Is it on me?"

You would never be late for work again. Not only would you be out of bed in a flash, but you'd be wide awake. And the furthest thing from your mind would be getting back into bed again. In fact, you'd just be elated that there was no vomit on you.

But the night our little boy woke us up sick was literally the night from hell. It was four in the morning, I was standing beside the bed in my underwear trying to focus my eyes, and my son was lying in the bed *laughing* in his own barf. From out of nowhere, the dog jumped up on the bed and started licking the baby.

"Get him off the bed!" my wife screamed.

So I reached for the boy.

"No! The dog, you idiot!" she yelled.

"My Lord, it's four in the morning, Honey," I tried to ratio-nalize. "Just let the dog clean him up. He can do it a heck of a lot better than we can. Besides, that's the happiest I've ever seen that dog."

My wife wasn't buying it. So we ended up doing it the hard way.

My son is happier now than I ever remember. It seems that about six months ago he *found* himself. I was getting ready to give him a bath, so I took off his little Power Ranger under-wear, and that's when it happened. He discovered himself. You couldn't have *bought* that kid a better present. In fact, I wish he'd have found himself before Christmas. He would have saved me 250 bucks.

"Merry Christmas, son. That's your tee-tee," I'd have said. "See ya on your birthday!"

He really loves that thing! Now, every bath time, we go through the same ritual: I take off his underwear, and he raises his arms and runs through the house laughing. He seems to enjoy the wind on his weenie, I guess. Lord, I don't know where he got *that* from!

One night in particular, while I was getting him ready for his bath, he took off his underwear and went running out of the bathroom. A few seconds later he walked back in holding him-self. He had this look on his face that said, "Dad, this is *so* cool!"

He just stood there squishing and squeezing it like Silly-

Putty. His face had an expression that I've only seen late at night in bars. He looked a little drunk. Then, he started stretching it. He must have thought he was Stretch Armstrong.

I said, "Easy Silly-Putty Boy, easy."

When my son was a newborn, my wife and I decided to have him circumcised. My daughter, who was five years old at the time, noticed the change in him immediately. She asked us what had happened.

Now, I have to admit, circumcision is a very difficult thing to explain to a five-year-old girl, because Barney hasn't come out with that book yet. You can't just say, "Well, Honey, we, uh, cut part of his weenie off. So be very glad you're a girl."

So we did the next best thing — we made something up.

Then, about two days later, I was about to change my son's diaper. My daughter walked into the room and said the strangest thing. She said, "Dad, I'd like to see the pee-pee of my brother, please." Like we keep it in a jar on the shelf or something.

So I removed the wet diaper and said, "Well, Baby, there it is. There's the pee-pee of your brother. In his hand, like it always is."

She looked at it for a second and said, "He's got an *ugly* pee-pee, Daddy."

"That's right, Pumpkin," I said. "Every man's pee-pee is ugly. Don't you ever forget that. They are mean, scary things. You see one, you kill it, okay? 'Cause if you don't, I'm gonna."

Having a baby around the house is quite an adventure. Fortunately, we'd been through it once before, but you know, it's never the same, is it? But there was one thing that was exactly the same with both kids: my wife decided to breast-feed both the babies. I think that this is a wonderful thing. Doctors all agree that it's the best way to start a youngster out in life, and there is no more wholesome picture than that of a mother feeding an infant in this most natural fashion. But the cool part is how a woman's breasts get so much bigger.

One night after the second baby was born, I got to feeling a little romantic and started kissing her on the neck and rubbing her back. She was enjoying the attention, but she turned and looked at me and said, "Look, Bill. This is all fine and good, but you can't touch my breasts."

I said, "What? You've got to be kidding!" Heck, that's like giving a kid a brand-new bike — with two flat tires. What good is that?

"I'm sorry, Honey, but they're sore," she explained, recognizing the hurt-child look on my face.

"Well," I countered. "How sore?"

She assured me they were far too sore for *any* sort of extra-curricular activity. Needless to say, I read myself to sleep that night.

Well, a few days later, idiot that I am, I decided to have some fun and get back at her. *She* got to feeling a little romantic and started kissing my neck and rubbing my back. I'll bet you can see where this is going, can't you?

Anyway, after a couple of minutes, I turned and looked at

her and said, "Look, Baby. This is all fine and good, but you
can't touch me down there because it's sore."

But instead of an argument, she just backed off and said,
"Okay."

Meanwhile I started whining that it wasn't *that* sore. All
right, I was *begging* by that time. And no, I'm not going to tell
you how this particular story ended. I might be stupid, but I've
got my pride! Or at least *some* pride.

THE DISCOVERY CHANNEL

I f you have kids, or even if you don't, you may find yourself spending a lot of time watching the Discovery Channel
on television. I love the Discovery Channel. My kids get to
watch programs on nature that they really enjoy and learn
about the world around us at the same time. It's wonderful. But
every now and then, I find myself wondering if maybe, just
maybe, we're trying to figure out way too much about certain
animals.

Last year my wife and I went for our first whale-watching
expedition off the coast of California. Let me tell you, it was
really cool. We got to see quite a few whales and got very close
to one in particular. And as we watched, the whale made a
high-pitched squealing noise.

Just then, everyone freaked out. They started jabbering
excitedly, saying stuff like, "What'd he say, what'd he say?"

I hollered, "He just said, 'Wheeeeep,' that's what he said.
Stop trying to figure stuff out!"

But I do think it would be really neat if someday we found out that whales could talk the same as you and me. Perhaps all these years, they have just been messing with us with those little squeals and squeaks. Wouldn't it be great to catch a couple of whales talking underneath the ocean.

"Man, you should've been here yesterday," one would say to the other. "There was this scuba diver, and I went, 'wheeeeee.' You won't believe this. He started *writing stuff down*! I laughed so hard I choked water in my blowhole!"

Face it, sometimes we just try too hard to understand the animal kingdom. But thanks to programming on networks like the Discovery Channel, I've learned an awful lot about animals that I just wouldn't have learned otherwise. Not that it makes a big difference in my life, but you never can tell when goofy animal trivia might come up at a cocktail party or something.

One thing I learned is that the frog really got the raw end of the deal. I mean, what do you and I do if we eat something we don't like? Real quick-like, we spit it out, right? But the poor frog has that sticky tongue. If he zaps something nasty, it stays zapped until he swallows it.

I'm convinced that when you hear frogs croaking at night, it's just their way of saying, "Aw, man! This tastes like crap!" And there's nothing they can do about it but moan.

I saw a show the other day called "Animals of the Sahara Desert." It was absolutely fascinating. Okay, it wasn't boring. Anyway, they showed a segment on this desert wasp that spends its whole life digging a hole in the sand for its mate. And she just stands there and *watches*. All right, so maybe she stands there griping at him, like "Honey, when you've finished there, I want a pool!"

But the bottom line is that the male *dies* while he's still digging this hole. Now I don't know about you, but if it was me, after like an hour of digging, I'd be thinking, "You know, Darlin', you're getting uglier by the minute, I can tell you that right now. You want a pool? Well, I wanted a mate with big antennae!"

During the course of the program, they said that the sands of the Sahara Desert get to be around 150°F. One type of lizard that lives there doesn't move around when his feet get too hot; he just lifts them up, like he's running in place. It's kind of like playing that old kid's game "Hot Potato" all by yourself. He just dances around like a rock star, and never goes anywhere. And you know if he could talk, he'd be saying something like, "Wheweee, this sand is hot!"

And while I was watching, I just kept thinking, for all that moving around and him not going anywhere, why doesn't he find some shade?

I guess they don't make *signs* small enough for lizards, but maybe they should.

Some other interesting critters that live in the desert are these bugs whose whole job in life is just to run. That's it. Run. They form up in a straight line and just book-it across the desert. They're not going anywhere in particular; they just go. It's like one of them wakes up in the morning and calls out to the others, "Hey! Y'all ready to go?" And the others say, "Hit it, Buddy. We're right behind you! Hey, let's run past that lizard.

He's hilarious!"

And there's a certain kind of snake that eats those bugs. Now, he can't sit on top of the sand because they'd see him. So he burrows down and covers himself up, then *listens* for the bugs to come running past.

Can you just picture that snake hiding under the sand with his buddy. "Shhhhhh, shhhhh. Here they come. Yeah, that's them. Hear that one? He's got a limp. Hear it?"

That leads me to another question I've always wondered about. How do animals know which one is the weakest? You know, like when lions hunt zebras, they always go for the weak and the infirm. They always seem to know which is the weakest zebra. Well, how do they know that?

I have this theory. Now it's nothing scientific, mind you, but I figure there has to be a squealer-zebra. One little patsy-zebra that doesn't want to get eaten, so he narcs on all his buddies.

He'd go sneaking up to the lion's den, "Hey fellas," he'd whisper. "Now here's the deal: There's a herd of us a couple hundred yards down there. Now everybody's in pretty good shape — 'cept Bob."

Then he'd look around to make sure none of the other zebras were watching him. "Bob smokes. He'll be good for about fifty yards, then he'll start wheezing. That's when you guys can cut him out."

Like I said, it's just a theory.

SNAKES!!

Everyone I know seems to have at least one totally irrational fear. I mean, that *one thing* that just scares the living daylights out of them, but may not bother other people in the least. For some people it's the fear of flying or a fear of heights or water. But for me, there's no question, it's snakes.

That's right, snakes are the worst. I don't mind admitting that I'm afraid of snakes, because I know a lot of people are, and I like to think that we're the sane ones. As far as I'm concerned, they're the devil. I mean, hey, snakes can *move*, but they don't have any legs. That ain't right!

At least I know where my fear of snakes came from. It all goes back to when I was a little boy in Texas. One day my buddy and I were down at a farm pond, you know, messing around and doing "kid" stuff. We were skipping rocks, blowing fish up with M-80s, that kind of stuff. We were having a great time.

Next thing I know, my buddy catches this water snake by the tail. He jerks him out of the water and yells over to me: "Hey, look at this, Bill. Just look at him jiggle around!"

Then, my buddy started swinging him around and around. He thought that was really funny, and at that point, I was even enjoying it a little myself.

"Hey, you think he's gettin' dizzy?" he asked with that Texan-sincerity. Because, you know, Texans wonder about stuff like that.

Anyway, he whipped the snake around and around his head, and pretty soon it started to stretch out to about twice its normal length.

Now I've got to stop right here and ask a silly question. Have you ever known when somebody was about to do something really wicked, just by the look in his eye? Well, I saw that look right then in my buddy's eye, but before I had a chance to duck or run, he just let loose of that snake and tossed it right on me!

Well, heck yeah, I passed out.

I mean, it was either pass out or pee in my pants. And, at the time, passing out seemed the more manly thing to do. I don't know of anyone who would just stand there coolly and say, "A snake. Please stop it." It's hard to remain cool with a snake airborne at you, because they just don't fly right.

To this day, I still have nightmares about snakes. Have you ever had the one where you're lying in bed, it's late at night, and you have to go to the bathroom *really* bad? And the floor is just crawling with thousands of snakes. I'll tell you what, I just pee on myself. I am almost forty years old, but I couldn't give a darn. I'll wear the rubber pants. I'm not proud!

Yep, snakes are the worst. And do you know, before I got married, I dated this girl who had a snake for a pet. It was a twelve-foot boa constrictor she had named Fluffy. Well, that's just sick, in my book.

Anyway, it was our first date, and I didn't know about the snake. We had been out drinking, and truth is, we had *way* too much to drink. (Now I do not recommend this to anyone, but I was young and dumb, and didn't pay any attention to what my folks had told me.) But like I said, we had way too much to drink.

I was so drunk I had to keep looking at her belt to remember what her name was. Somehow or other, we ended up back at her mobile home. Lord, I wish I was making that part up, but it's true. She lived in one of the tiniest, single-wide trailer houses I'd ever seen. But at that point, I really didn't care. I was feeling pretty amorous, and she was looking better and better every minute.

(By the way, that is the same night I swore off tequila *forever*.)

So she closed the door behind us, then did her best Marilyn Monroe impression, "I'm gonna slip into something a little . . . more comfortable," she said with a quirky wink and what passed for a seductive smile.

Heck at that point, I'd have figured Ernest Borgnine was sexy, so it didn't really matter. I just said, "Alrighty!"

The way I saw it, I'd just stepped up to the plate and hit a home run! "I'll be waiting right here," I said as I staggered toward the sofa. "Or right here," I said as I stumbled and fell next to it. "Aw, heck, you'll see me."

After a few minutes, she came back from the bedroom/kitchen (and no, I'm not making that up either. I told you it was a *small* trailer.) This girl had on a sexy little negligée — and that *snake* wrapped around her neck.

Boy, that'll sober you up like a cold shower! In about two seconds, I was backing out the front door, sober as a judge, and thanking the good Lord that I was escaping with my life.

"No wait, Bill," she pleaded as I clawed my way through the screen door. "Fluffy can wrap around us while we make love."

With one foot sticking out the door, I gave her my best Humphrey Bogart sneer and said, "No, he can't. 'Cause I'll kill him."

With that, I ran from there as fast as I could, afraid that if I looked back she'd be swinging it around her head like a lasso. And she'd have that *look* in her eye.

I just can't imagine people who have snakes for pets. It just doesn't seem right, somehow. I heard about a family down in Florida who found a 30-foot python that weighed like 300 pounds, just living under their house!

How do you miss that? I mean, wouldn't your first clue be, "Honey, have you seen the dog?" And after a bit, "Honey?"

But you know, my little experience with Fluffy gave me an incredibly good idea to keep folks from ever drinking-and-driving again. Just have the cops carry snakes. Can you imagine?

You get a little buzzed, and the cops pull you over.

"You drunk, man?" the officer would say. "Here's a snake . . ." and he'd toss it in your lap. In the next few seconds, as you scramble to protect all that is dear, pee in your pants, and curse in tongues, you would find yourself amazingly sober.

"Heck no, I'm not drunk . . . not anymore. I just peed it all out." And after you bail out of the car and animal control goes in looking for the snake, you'd turn to the cop and beg him to just shoot you in the head next time.

Picture the rednecks hanging out in the neighborhood tavern.

"Hey, Bubba, you want a beer, man?"

"Heck no! Them cops is carryin' snakes now. I don't want no parts of that, man."

And one big greasy guy in the back would tip his Coke bottle up and chime in with, "They threw a cobra on Jimmy. That boy still ain't right."

And you know, of all the snakes, I think the cobra is the one I'd hate to get bit by the worst. Because the cobra will spit on you first, then bite you.

Well, I'm sorry, but that is a bunch of bull! Either bite me or leave me alone, all right? Don't humiliate me by spitting on me. I mean, I can get *that* in a bar.

PETS

I'm sure many of you have pets. I was brought up around pets and have always had at least one or two of God's creatures running around the house. I figure most folks fall into either one of two categories where pets are concerned; they are either "cat" people or they are "dog" people.

Okay, I know there are a whole bunch of people out there that have other rare and exotic pets, like lizards or miniature pigs. But, except maybe in California, owners of exotic pets are a very small minority. And I don't include horses or farm animals in this category, because I was always taught that those animals are not pets. They serve a useful purpose. By definition, a pet doesn't do anything productive. A pet just sits around looking dumb, eating and making a mess on your rug.

So, for all of you exotic pet owners out there, you might just want to skip ahead to the next chapter. There's nothing here that pertains to you, and it's just possible we may be talking about you behind your back.

Anyway, back to my theory about pet owners. I figure most people either prefer dogs or prefer cats. Unfortunately, they often inter-marry, and the result is that you get both kinds of pets running around the house. I hate to admit it, but the Engvall home is one such example.

Having both dogs and cats running around is a very interesting study in animal behavior. One of the most classic examples of the difference between cat and dog behavior is obvious when you come back from the vet after having your pet neutered. Dogs seem to understand, at least a little.

"All right, all right, all right!" they might say, upset but resigned to their fate. "I just *knew* something like this was gonna happen. Dang it!" And they might lick themselves a bit too often, but otherwise they quickly return to their old loveable selves shortly after their first feeding.

But if you neuter a cat, you'd better be ready for the guilt-trip of your life! When we brought our cat home from the vet, he started dragging his butt on the carpet. He doesn't actually *talk*, but we knew what he was thinking. "Just look at me! You *bastards*! What's missing from this picture? What am I gonna tell my friends?"

And if you have a cat, I'm sure you've made this mistake at least once. When you're lying in bed, and you think your cat is asleep, you move your feet underneath the covers.

"Mouse!" the cat hisses, as it sails directly on top of your foot, teeth and claws bared.

It doesn't seem to matter how hard you sling that cat against the wall, it never seems to stun him, does it? Nope, he just bounces off with that little attitude.

"So that's how we're gonna play, eh Buddy-boy?" the cat

says after he picks himself up again. "You'd best be sure and check your boots in the morning, big man. I believe you might just find a little present waitin' for you!"

My wife went crazy with her cat. She decided to teach it all sorts of tricks, like it was a *dog* or something. She taught this cat to go to the bathroom *in the toilet*. Do you know how bizarre that is? Imagine stumbling into the bathroom at, say, five in the morning, flipping on the light, and finding a furry little creature smiling up at you from the toilet seat.

After I pulled myself off the ceiling, I realized it was just the cat.

"Oh, hi Kitty," I mumbled, trying to cover my shock.

The cat looked up from his newspaper and said, "Hey, Bill. What's happening? Boy, this Garfield's a hoot, ain't he?"

What could I say?

I am a dog person myself, but to tell you the truth, I have one of the *stupidest* dogs in the world. All right, I know what you're thinking . . . and it was *purely* by coincidence. Anyway, if the doorbell rings, Max doesn't bark, he just pees all over everything. It may not be as effective as barking, but it *does* get our attention.

"Good boy, good boy, I'll get that door now."

And when he's not getting excited and peeing all over, Max is leaving piles around the house. I swear, he's like a finely tuned crapping-machine. Sometimes, I actually think he's possessed. Most nights he'll wake me up by tugging at the covers.

"Psssst! Hey, Bill," he'd say as I struggle to pop open one

eye. "It's okay. You don't need to get up to take me outside. I just crapped on the rug. Nighty-night."

What can you do? I usually just say, "Hey thanks, man. Appreciate your honesty. Good night."

Our dogs are mostly indoor dogs, which I don't mind too much except when my wife and I get a little romantic, and the dogs *watch* us. Now, I know they're just dogs, but it's just disconcerting as heck. Face it, it's hard to be romantic when there's this pair of eyes peering up over the edge of the bed. You can almost hear what they're thinking: "Whooooweee! Nice move there, Bill. But doesn't that hurt your back? Hey, Max just crapped on the rug again."

Sometimes, I try to be a little, you know, spontaneous. I might toss my underwear across the room, and the dogs bring them back. Or worse, they get into a tug-of-war with them which escalates into a full-fledged fight. Boy, nothing will break a romantic mood faster than having to jump up and pull two snarling dogs apart.

We bought our daughter a puppy, and at the time it seemed like a pretty good idea. Here's a hint, folks. Don't ever do that. Don't ever buy a seven-year-old anything live, because she'll just kill it.

We bought her a miniature long-haired dachshund — a wiener dog. Well, actually, it's so small it's more like a cocktail-frank dog. And this dog has not walked since we've owned it. My daughter either carries it or pushes it around in a baby carriage.

I've tried to reason with her like, "Baby, please let the dog walk."

She just snaps her hands on her hips and says, "Dad, he *needs* me to carry him."

And the poor dog is giving me that look like, "Just kill me, Bill. For heaven's sake, I'm not even a dog any more. Look at me, I'm wearing Barbie jeans, for crying out loud."

They say that for a dog, one human year is like seven dog years. For our little wiener dog, I think it's more like every day is a year. Pretty soon he'll figure out how to hide under the couch like the rest of the animals, and then he'll be all right.

AIRPLANES!

Unfortunately in my job I am required to fly quite a bit. I say "unfortunately," because there are very few things in this world that scare me, but flying is one of them. I know it's an irrational fear, but that makes no difference.

The thing that bothers me most about my fear of flying is that I have no idea *why* I'm afraid. At least with my other irrational fear, the fear of snakes, I can recall a very frightening incident that *caused* the fear. Not so with flying. I'm just plain scared, and I don't know why.

Maybe it's the death-thing that scares me, or simply just not being able to control my own destiny. At least if you are driving a car, you can slam on the brakes, swerve to the side of the road or something. Even if some drunk plows into you, as the driver of car-B did (that's what the police report said), you can feel as if you have at least some say in whether or not you survive.

Maybe they should install a little flight yoke, like the pilot has, at each seat. Not a real one, of course, just something like infant play cars have. A little plastic steering wheel, with maybe a horn or something, so people who are afraid can *pretend* to be in control. And maybe, instead of showing a movie, they can hook up a video monitor that would show us the view out the front window. That way, we can actually *see* the mountain we are about to hit. Then, we can all yank on our little plastic flight yokes, and pull the airplane safely over the top. Or at least our screams will wake up the pilot, and *he* can save our lives.

Another big difference between flying and driving, I guess, is that most car accidents are not fatal. It pretty much has to be your time to go, the way I see it.

I guess what really bothers me is, if the plane were to crash, what if it wasn't really *my* time? What if I just got on the plane by mistake, and it was the *other people* who are on the plane with me whose numbers got called? The thought of death by association just doesn't appeal to me.

To help pass the time while flying, I started studying people and their habits on airplanes. Man, there is a definite need for *Stupid signs* on airplanes!

One thing I have learned is that most people must check their brains with their luggage. That is *when* they check their luggage. Apparently it has become very chic to carry on as much luggage as you can. I won't be surprised at all if it soon becomes an Olympic event.

". . . Well, there's Jethro," an announcer would say. "He's got five pieces of luggage, weighing an incredible 600 pounds. But wait, the gate attendant has noticed that one of the bags will not fit under the seat. He'll have to check that bag! Oh, too bad, Jethro. And he was so close to setting a new record...."

Anyway, I guess the logic most folks use is that, if they don't check any bags, they won't have to wait around at baggage claim, and there's almost no chance of their luggage going to Maui while they go to Cleveland. But if you're one of these people, let me clue you in on a little secret. Think about this, if *everyone* checked their bags, boarding would only take a few minutes. Find your seat, sit down. That's it. The plane would leave on time and, at your destination, deplaning would be just as quick.

While I wish more people would check their luggage instead of packing it into the overhead compartment, I can *almost* understand it. I don't *agree* with it, but I understand it. However, there is no understanding the couple who bring on the Baby-Stroller-from-Hell and try to roll it down the aisle.

Without a doubt, people who insist on wheeling Junior down the narrow aisle of an airplane deserve *signs*. Big ones.

Let's break this down to its bare facts. Here is this lovely couple and their child. The child probably weighs no more than 12 pounds at the most. However, the parents feel they cannot carry that child a mere 50 feet.

Heck, Dad's carry-on bag probably weighs more than the kid. Why not get a stroller for the bag? Oh wait, what am I thinking? They *do* have strollers for luggage. Those little wheeled carts that only flight attendants had for a while? And now, *everybody's* got one.

Yeah, please stick that metal-wheeled cart in the overhead storage bin. That way, when it flies open, I can look forward to a nice head contusion!

I am a firm believer that all prospective airline passengers should have to attend an airplane familiarity course before they are allowed to board the first time. Graduates could then be given little cards with their pictures on them they could use over and over again. Those who fail the course could be given what they really needed in the first place, *Stupid signs.*

For example, there's inevitably someone whose seat number is like, 34A. He steps into the cabin, stops at a first-class seat then looks at his ticket and compares it to the seat number on the overhead. See, if people like that had to wear *Stupid signs,* the flight attendants could just walk them back to their seats without holding up all the folks behind them.

What if they started numbering seats from the back of the plane forward? That might be a neat little gimmick for some airline to try. Imagine if the last row of seats in the tail of the plane were number 1. And the first-class seats were like, rows 34–37.

"Yes, sir," the ticket agent would say. "I can confirm you a seat in 1-A." Who wouldn't jump at that?

The other thing about flying that really gets under my skin is that no one listens to the flight attendants or the pilots when they make their announcements. It's no wonder that when planes go down so few people get out.

A good example of this is when the plane is taxiing up to the gate. The pilot always says, "Please, stay in your seat until the fasten-seatbelt sign goes off." What happens? Invariably somebody has to jump up to get his carry-on luggage, to make sure he is the first one off the plane.

See, if I could, I would like to work for the airlines. It would be my job to make sure that everyone obeys and understands the rules. The way it would work is like this: I would dress in street clothes, like an undercover cop, and carry around the skinny part of a fishing rod. You know, the part that is real flexible. Now if someone did something stupid, like jumping up when the plane was still taxiing, I would pop him on the neck with that fishing rod. That way it would leave a red mark and everyone would know that the guy had screwed up on an airplane. Oh, by the way, I would also hand him an *I'm Stupid* sign.

I don't know what has happened to the meal service on airlines, but apparently it is nonexistent anymore.

I was on a flight the other day going to Ft. Lauderdale. When we were starting to board, the gate agent informed us that we were on a "bistro" flight. Bistro? When I think of the word *bistro*, I think of a French cafe with coffee that could have powered Apollo-13 home.

Not anymore. Apparently *bistro*, to this particular airline anyway, means "sack lunch." I am not kidding you, it was a sack lunch! There was a rock-hard roll, split in half, with some kind of meat surprise in the middle, a bag of chips and a cookie. I pack a better lunch for my kids to take to school.

Oh, well, what do you expect for a $400 plane ticket?

Finally, we get to the *real* issue of flying: SAFETY. It seems that recently there has been a rash of accidents. This scares me to death, so to speak.

There was a flight from Los Angeles that had to abort its take-off because another jet pulled in front of it. Now let's think about this. I understand the possibility that the flight controller might have made a mistake, or perhaps the errant pilot may have not heard the flight controllers command correctly. But, what I don't get is, how the pilot did not *see* the other jet!

I mean how big is a jet? About as big as a house, right? Let's face facts; it's not like a stray dog darted out in front of the jet. I can just imagine the conversation in the cockpit:

"Okay Jim, we've been cleared for take-off."

"Hey look out! There's another plane right there!"

"Man, I didn't even *see* him! He came right out of the bushes . . ."

Another incident that happened when a plane crashed in Dallas on take-off, and, fortunately, many of the passengers survived the crash. The people that survived the crash were then put on *another* jet with the same company. Then, *that* plane had to abort its take-off because of engine problems.

You know that those people had to be thinking, "Hey, I've got an idea! Why don't you just *shoot* us in the head? It would be a lot quicker and a lot more humane than this."

And then, there was a plane that had to land without any landing gear. Great! Now we've got pilots *power sliding* into airports.

This made me wonder where they put animals on the airplane. You got it: underneath. You know those animals had to be thinking, "Hey! Hey, hey! This ain't right, Fluffy. I'm telling you, something is wrong. My toenails are gone!"

Oh well, what can you do? Just grab your little sack lunch and hope that everything goes well, and that you're not on a flight with someone whose number is up.

State Fairs

In the past few years, I have been very fortunate to have opened for some very big and very talented country acts, which I enjoyed immensely. However, it's not all glitter and bright lights. When you go on the road with a country musician you are eventually going to wind up playing at a state fair, enjoying the sights, sounds and *smells* of the country.

Now don't get me wrong, I love a state fair as much as the next guy, but here's a little tip for you. If you've ever had one of those mornings when you woke up and just didn't feel good about yourself, I have just the solution to your problem. What you need to do is go to a state fair and just look around.

I am not kidding! I've seen people at state fairs that could be their own *dads*. Yep, you start feeling bad about yourself, you just go to a state fair, and in just a few short minutes of looking around, you'll get to thinking just how fortunate you really are.

The *outfits* people wear to state fairs! I've seen people wearing

clothes that I would not have worn to pick up dog mess out of
the backyard! And I am by no means a member of the fashion
elite. But some of these people look like they pick their clothes
out of a dumpster behind the quick-mart.

One guy I remember was wearing a T-shirt that said, "MY
WIFE'S A WITCH" and a ball cap that said, "WHO FART-
ED?" At the time I was thinking, this guy is probably someone's *dad*! What kind of example is he setting for his kid? It
was frightening. But, do you want to know what was even
scarier? I got to looking around and realized that he wasn't the
only one. There was a whole *herd* of them. They're breeding!

On a recent concert tour we stopped at the Iowa State Fair. If
you've never been there, this is one awesome fair. It is one of
the largest state fairs in the country, and literally hundreds of
thousands of people pass through the gates every day. And
while they have all the traditional fair stuff, they also have
some unique and unusual displays, too.

One of the more memorable novelties I recall was a six-foot
statue of Garth Brooks, carved out of *butter*. It was amazing,
yet somehow very strange. It made me wonder about the lady
who carved it. When did she realize she had that ability to
carve butter? It probably started at the dinner table.

"Hey, Mom! That's a dang fine dog you carved out of the
butter bar."

"Well, thank you, Jimmy."

"You know you ought to go on to something bigger. That
Garth Brooks is a nice-lookin' fella."

My question is *why*? Why would you carve a six-foot statue of Garth Brooks out of butter? The only thing I could think of was that lady had way too much time on her hands.

And the shame of it is, as wonderful as that statue was, all they were going to do was melt it down. That poor woman who carved Garth out of butter, well, who'd ever believe her? She'd be at a party somewhere, bragging to her friends, "I carved a six-foot statue of Garth Brooks out of butter."

"Bull——!"

"I sure did."

"Well, where is it?"

"Oh, they melted it down, and poured it on that popcorn statue of Alan Jackson."

While we were at the Iowa State Fair, I saw was a man selling rocks. Rocks! He'd painted two eyes and a smile on them. Now how many people do you think walked by his booth and said, "Honey, we ain't got one smiling rock at our house. Reckon we ought to pick one up?"

I think that's what scares me the most about retirement, you have a lot of time to build stuff no one wants.

I also got to perform at the Minnesota State Fair. It's even bigger than the Iowa State Fair, I think. It was at this fair that I saw a guy selling blow-guns, for kids. We're talking real African blow-guns with little metal darts.

I couldn't resist. I walked up to him and said, "How can you sell these to kids?"

"Hey pal, we give 'em a styrofoam target!" he answered, looking me right in the eye.

Ohhhhh, okay. That's different, 'cause we all know the *first* place a kid is gonna point that blow-gun is at a *styrofoam target*, right? Well, I don't think so! Grandma's fat butt, yes. A styrofoam target, no, probably not.

It was also at the Minnesota State Fair that I saw this woman. God bless her, she must have weighed 1,500 pounds. I am not lying, either.

The weight-guessing guy just said, "No." He shook his head solemnly. "You don't really want me hollerin' that number out, do you?"

You know what the problem was? It wasn't that she was *big.* Big doesn't bother me at all. What bothered me was, in one hand she had a funnel cake with every condiment in the world on it. Mustard, mayonnaise, even dirt from the ground was on this thing. In her mouth, she was holding a burrito like a cigarette, and in her other hand she had a roasted ear of corn.

All I could think was, "Good God, if you *look* like that, don't go to a fair and *eat* like that." Because, you know, there was not one single person at that fair thinking, "Awww, I bet she's just got a thyroid problem."

But, you know what the funniest thing about it was? Hanging on to this very large woman was a bean-pole-skinny, 80-pound man, just *begging* for scraps.

"You gonna eat the husk off that corn, Punkin'?"

To which she replied, "Shut up, I'll feed you when it's time. Now go get Momma some cotton candy — and a Diet Coke!"

I saw one man at the fair, chunking quarters into a booth so he could play Tic-Tac-Toe against a chicken. Now how sad is that? I'll tell you how sad it is, not only does this man have no life at all, but he's *never* gonna win. Because if the chicken loses, it gets an electric shock! Now *that's* motivation!

I don't know about you, but if you shock *me* a couple of times with high voltage I am gonna *learn* whatever it is you want. But there he was, hollering at his wife to get him another roll of quarters, because no stupid chicken was gonna beat *him*.

God bless you, sir, and here's your official *I'm Stupid* sign.

At every fair I have ever been to, there has usually been some kind of carnival attached. I've always loved carnivals — the midway; the House of Mirrors, not a great place to discover you're claustrophobic; caramel apples; and, of course, who can forget, the freak shows.

It's funny how most people won't even look directly at a bag person in Los Angeles, but they'll pay a buck to go see "The Lizard Boy."

The only thing I have *never* been a big fan of at the carnival is the rides. If it spins, rotates, or goes upside down, these are what I call the "Puke and Barf" rides.

I recently took my son on a ride called "The Scrambler." I am sure most of you have been on this ride. Its big deal is centrifugal force, which is another no-no in Bill's book. But I didn't want to disappoint my son, so we got on the ride.

Once we were seated, I noticed it had a big bolt sticking out, and the nut was just spinning around on the end of it. I thought, "That ain't right." So I tried to get the attendant's attention. Of course, that was when I got my first really good look at him. I have to say, his outward appearance did not instill a great deal of confidence in me. However, I saw his name tag which proclaimed that his name was Earl (go figure).

So, anyway, there I was, trying to get Earl's attention, which was about as simple as getting a shot of tequila at an AA dance. Much to my chagrin, the ride started without warning.

Falling victim to the enormous centrifugal force, I quickly found myself smashing my son into the corner of the seat. While trying to pull myself off of him, so he could breathe, I continued yelling at Earl, "Slow down! Slow this darned thing down!"

However, my pleas must have sounded to Earl like, "Let's see just how fast this puppy will go!" I'm now convinced that ride operators must get paid a bonus every time someone pukes on their ride.

After the ride had ended and the security guards had peeled me off Earl, I casually walked over to the trash can and lost everything I had eaten for the last six months. It really pained me to give Earl the satisfaction (and the cash bonus), but I didn't have any choice.

As we walked away I heard Earl hollering joyously, "He blew in cart four! That's another hundred bucks!"

"Sorry, son," I said by way of explaining my actions. "Remind Daddy to put on his *sign* when we get home."

MARRIAGE

Human beings, as with all of God's other creatures, are driven from birth toward that ultimate goal of procreation. Most civilized human cultures recognize the institution of marriage as the easiest and most logical way to mate, and thus begin the wonderful cycle of life with a new generation of offspring.

Marriage has never been easy. And through the years, people have sought to glorify the institution in order to make it more attractive to young people. We simply call this "brainwashing." It starts in the cradle. From the time we are infants and our parents read fairy tales to us, don't they all end with, "and they were married and lived happily ever after"?

In our society today, we figure "happily married" means neither spouse has called the cops to settle a dispute in the past six months. And that's a shame, but it's true. If you were born in the fifties or sixties, you grew up with such great television shows as "Ozzie & Harriet" or "The Brady Bunch" or "The Dick Van

Dyke Show," on which families could laugh at their problems, but always overcame them. Divorce was never even considered.

Today, divorce is almost planned for. It's like people are getting married with the attitude that, "Heck, we'll give this a shot, and if it doesn't work, we'll just call it off." And that to me is just really sad. See, I was raised to believe that marriage was a lifelong commitment, to spouse and children, and that divorce should be the very last option you choose.

Knowing this very early on, I decided to select my mate very carefully. And after searching and searching, I found just the right woman when I was in college. She was beautiful, had a great figure, and had a wonderful sense of humor. In fact, there was only one thing about her I considered less than perfect — she refused to have anything to do with *me*. (I guess I should add *intelligent* to her list of attributes.)

But I was persistent. I knew a good thing when I saw it, and I knew that she was *the one* for me. I never gave up and when I was 24 years old, she finally agreed to become my bride.

I was the happiest man on earth, but, right from the beginning, I started getting suspicious. I had this nagging little feeling that things were not going to be exactly the way they were on television marriages. I began to notice subtle things all around me that should have warned me of things to come, but I was a hopeless romantic, and deeply in love.

The first thing I noticed was that, when we told people we were getting married, everyone had some "wonderful advice" on how to make it work. Disturbingly, most of the advice came from people who were divorced. I started to get the feeling that this marriage-thing wasn't going to be everything I had figured.

But the real wake-up call for me didn't come until a few days after the honeymoon. I was quite surprised at all the little things that were suddenly different.

Not that they were all bad changes, mind you. Some of them were pretty nice changes, but they were *changes* nonetheless, things I would just have to learn to get used to. I wish someone would just sit down and write a book called, *Things That Change When You Get Married*. It would make it so much easier for young couples to adjust.

The first change I noticed was that the water in our toilet turned this beautiful shade of blue. It looked like that water down in the Caribbean. I halfway expected to hear some island music when I lifted the lid.

Another thing I noticed about my new married life was that the whole house started smelling better. And that was a good thing. I never knew if it was the subtle hint of her perfume that seemed to linger everywhere, or the fact that she pulled all my dirty sweat socks out from under the sofa, or the fact that she actually *washed* every dish in the house.

Yep, quite a few things change once that ring hits the finger. I never thought I would learn to hate the sound of my own name, but there are times when I do.

"Bill?"

"Oh, Bill?"

I know it's not going to be "Oh, Bill do you want 50 bucks?" More like, "Bill, will you take out the garbage?" or "Bill, don't forget you're cleaning the gutters this Saturday," or "Oh, Bill, you forgot to put the toilet seat down again!"

I'm convinced that one of the reasons my wife and I have

stayed together for the past thirteen years is that we don't play board games together. We learned *that* early on.

We once tried playing that game called *Pictionary*. You know, where you have to *draw clues* on a piece of paper, so your partner can guess the word. My Lord, by the time the game was over, we had lawyers on the phone! As I recall, the men were winning, but just by a tiny bit. The ladies needed only *one word* to win the game, and my wife was the guesser. I swear, it happened just this way. Her partner drew a straight line — a *straight line*! My wife immediately yelled, "Hydroponic farm?" Incredibly, the *right* answer!

The women were shrieking, "Yes! We win! Yes, yes . . ." while the guys were looking around like a UFO had just landed in the living room. Then one of the guys finally said aloud what we were all thinking: "How'd she get that?"

"Meet Mrs. Milton Bradley," I said sarcastically.

That was the last time we ever played board games together. I mean, in the ensuing argument, after everyone left for home, we weren't just considering *divorce*, we were actually talking custody arrangements! It just isn't worth it.

When my wife and I first got married, like many young couples, we were on a very tight budget. Being thrifty, my wife became a coupon clipper. In those days, I loved her all the more for it. But *now*, I will pay *whatever* the groceries cost. Just please, oh please, don't make me use coupons.

On Sunday morning, you don't mess with my wife. She sits in the middle of the living room and those scissors just *fly*! With scraps of paper floating around the room like confetti, she screams stuff like, "Creamed corn, 50 cents off! Artichoke hearts, two for a dollar! I don't *believe* this."

But the worst part is when we get to the grocery store. We fill a cart with enough groceries to feed the Partridge family, and then, in the check-out line, she whips out this encyclopedia-size *book* of coupons. And wouldn't you know there's always a guy in line behind us moaning, "I just wanna get these grapes. They're gonna be *raisins* by the time this chick is done!"

One key to a happy marriage is learning to do things that the other person likes, and, in theory, this is a great idea. The problem is that my wife likes to do macramé. I am sorry, there are a lot of things I will do, but macramé is not one of them.

She made the stupidest thing I have ever seen. Have you ever seen that little owl that everyone, it seems, macramés? You know the one, with the little round eyes and the stick through his head and feet? It's hanging in our den.

Now, I like to fish, and my wife hates to. She says she gets bored. But I didn't realize how bored she got until I caught her trying to set the minnows free. I heard her saying, "You're free! Go, go, little fishies! Quick, here he comes!"

Of course on that excursion she caught not only the biggest fish, but she caught the *only* fish. And then what did she do? She swung the fish over into my face and asked *me* to take the fish off the hook.

You see, the way I was raised if you *caught* the fish, *you* took it off the hook. Well, apparently that doesn't hold true when you are fishing with your wife.

But, with my *sign* securely tied about my neck, I decided to try and convince her that she should take the fish off by herself. I mean, the way I saw it, it was bad enough that she caught the only fish, but to ask me to take it off the hook was just like rubbing my nose in it. My *pride* was hurt.

So I casually looked her in the eye and said, "Honey, if you'll touch this," I pointed to my lap, "then, why won't you touch that fish?"

"Because the fish is bigger," she replied without hesitation.

Which leads me to consider sex. Heck, for that matter I am *always* considering sex. But for now, we'll just settle for *discussing* sex and marriage.

Sex changes after you get married, and, in my opinion, it gets better the longer you're married. Now I know, at this point, you might think I have completely lost my mind, but hear me out.

I have been married now to the same woman for thirteen years. And one of the reasons that we have stayed together so long is we have a thing that I call "Love Magic."

Now "Love Magic" is not something you can just go down to the drugstore and buy. "Love Magic" is that certain something that two people have together that keeps them a little in awe of each other no matter what they're doing.

If you are lucky enough to have this magic already, hang on to it. It is one of the neatest things you will ever possess. And it doesn't matter what your mate is doing. Sometimes when my wife is mowing the yard, I get all emotional and choked up, and say things like, "I love you baby . . . but you missed a little spot there, didn't you?"

One of the hardest things for any couple to admit is that either one has laughed during sex. And we have all laughed during that little romantic moment, haven't we? I recall this one night when my wife and I were involved in a particularly hot session (only because it was August in Texas, which is like having sex in a Chinese steam pot).

Anyway, our bodies got sweaty on our stomachs and made one of those noises — you know, the kind of noise you used to make with your hand under your arm pit. I laughed so hard I thought I'd puke all over the bed. Needless to say, the moment was lost and we *read* each other to sleep that night.

Once we were having a little interlude and it was hot, I mean hot, hot, hot, hot, hot. My wife was arching her back and moaning, and all I could say was "Yes ma'am, You *are* welcome! I'm really turning you on, huh?"

"No, you idiot!" she yelled, "You're pulling my hair! Owwww."

Oh well, another manly dream shot to heck. It would never happen that way in the movies. You see, that's why I hate love scenes in movies. They don't portray it as it really is.

If two characters are gonna make love in the movies, they are naked in about a *second*. Their hair doesn't ever move, their makeup never smears, and they've got the perfect music that lasts the whole duration.

Heck, even I could be great if I had an *orchestra* following me around the house. I would just turn to the conductor and say, "Follow me, boys; we're heading to the shed."

But real life is not like that for you and me. When *real* people are making love, their hair is matted to their heads, the woman's mascara is smeared back to her ear. Heck, the man probably still has his underwear hanging on one ankle. You know, just that hot monkey love! Now that's something you'll *never* see in the movies!

My favorite love scene in the movies is what I call the "angry-passionate scene." If you saw the movie *Sea of Love*, you saw angry passion. When that fellow grabbed that woman's panties and just *ripped* them off her. I thought to myself, "I am gonna try that at my house."

Well, let me clue you in — it doesn't happen that way. The only way you can rip panties off a woman is if there is a hole already in them. If there's no hole, all you're going to do is jerk on her underwear.

When I tried it, I remember my wife looking at me and saying, "What are you *doing*?"

"Being sexy!" I replied confidently.

"Well, thanks for the *wedgie*, Romeo," she said as she tried to undo the damage I had wrought. "Now dial 911. I think you dislocated my hip."

Like I said, sex in the movies just isn't real, but it does give us ordinary humans some wonderful ideas sometimes. And sometimes not.

We saw *9 1/2 weeks*. Lord, now there's another movie I should not have watched. There was a scene in which Mickey Rourke fed a woman fruit. It was so sexy I nearly came out of my seat. And the great part was, it looked so simple I thought even *I* could do it, in the comfort and privacy of my own bedroom.

So, we went home and I told my wife to go into the bedroom and get ready because *this* was going to be wild. Then I headed off to the kitchen to get the "props." When I opened the refrigerator door, however, much to my dismay, there was no fruit. Not being one to be easily deterred, I rounded up some *other* forms of food.

Let me take a moment here to share a little advice with the newlyweds, or any couple for that matter, trying to spice up the bedroom. Bologna and string cheese are *not* a big turn-on to a blindfolded woman. You'll have to trust me on this one!

Another of my favorite love scenes in the movies is the one in which the couple is rolling wildly around the bed. I mean, sheets and pillows are flying, and then they roll off the bed and hit the floor. And they keep right on going without missing a beat.

Well, *I am sorry*, but that just doesn't happen! If you roll off the bed onto your partner, what do you hear?

"Owwwww! Get off me, you idiot! I swear, you just broke my back!"

To which the men usually reply, "Sorry. Uhh . . . can you go some more?"

I guess what all this is leading up to is this: One of the things that bothers me about this country is we are too uptight about sex. The bedroom is where some of the funniest stuff happens.

And when it does, *laugh out loud*.

Trust me, if you can get past the uptightness of sex, sex is very funny. And I just happen to have a great example.

Three years ago on my wife's birthday, I had it planned to a tee! I had a bottle of Dom Perignon chilled by the edge of the bed, candles on the headboard, and some soft country music playing. Let me tell you something, we really got *into* it.

I mean, it was just that "Hot-Pig-Sex." You know the kind I'm talking about. After a couple of beers, you get so into it, that you make one of those pig-snorting noises. But no one notices, or cares. You're just rooting around, like a pig at the trough.

Well, we forgot about the *candles*. Apparently, the headboard was doing some serious moving, because hot wax splashed onto my chest. I screamed like a woman who has just seen the psycho-killer in a horror movie.

My wife, her eyes still closed in ecstasy, just smiled and said, "Yes, sir! You *are* welcome!"

ABOUT THE AUTHORS

Among **Bill Engvall's** impressive credits are the American Comedy Award for Best Male Stand-Up in 1992 and a recurring role as Buck Overton on the television show "Delta," starring Delta Burke. His more recent accomplishments include *Here's Your Sign*, a comedy album released by Warner Bros. in May 1996, and the role of Bill Pelton on NBC's "The Jeff Foxworthy Show." He lives in Los Angeles with his wife and children.

David Brown, author of *Gold Buckle Dreams,* lives in Sparks, Nevada.